Original title:
Whispers of Snow

Author: Linda Leevike
ISBN HARDBACK: 978-9916-79-753-2
ISBN PAPERBACK: 978-9916-79-754-9
ISBN EBOOK: 978-9916-79-755-6

Chilly Secrets in the Air

Whispers ride the frosty breeze,
Veiled murmurs of what once was.
Footsteps crunch on hidden dreams,
Frozen tales beneath the thaw.

Branches bare, their secrets keep,
Underneath the silver sky.
Nature holds its breath in peace,
Chilly secrets never die.

Echoes Beneath the Ice

Silent cries from depths below,
Memories trapped in crystal chains.
Echoes resonate through the cold,
Stories lost in winter's reins.

Shadows dance on frozen lakes,
Ripples fade where none have tread.
Voices murmur in twilight haze,
In the stillness, echoes spread.

Gentle Crystals Ascend

Snowflakes drift from heaven’s hand,
Each a gem in twilight's glow.
Whirling softly, they mend the land,
In their embrace, the world will slow.

Gentle crystals, pure and bright,
Carpet dreams in purest white.
Kisses from the skies above,
Wrapping earth in winter's love.

A Blanket of Quietude

A stillness wraps the sleeping ground,
Nature paused in a soft sigh.
Whispers fade, no single sound,
Only snowflakes softly fly.

In this hush, the heart finds peace,
Melodies of silence play.
With each flake, the world's release,
A blanket softening the day.

Lullabies of the Snowbound Night

Whispers dance in silver light,
Snowflakes glide, so soft and white.
A hush envelops all that's near,
Embracing hearts, dispelling fear.

Dreams of warmth in winter's breath,
Snowy blankets cradle death.
In this stillness, peace is found,
With lullabies of night profound.

Glimmers of the Snowfall's Voice

The world adorned in icy grace,
Each flake a gem, a fleeting trace.
Beneath the stars, a quiet song,
Hope whispers where we all belong.

Shimmering where shadows play,
Winter's light holds night at bay.
In glimmers soft, the silence speaks,
Of tender joys the heart still seeks.

Shrouded in Frosted Dreams

Covered paths in glistening sheen,
A tranquil world, serene, unseen.
Frosted dreams weave through the night,
Painting visions, pure delight.

Moonbeams dance on icy streams,
Nature hums her quiet themes.
Beneath the icy, starry veil,
Whispers of stories long since pale.

The Winter's Gentle Secrets

Underneath the frozen sky,
Winter guards its secrets nigh.
In crystal whispers, truth is spun,
Tales of warmth when day is done.

Silent echoes in the frost,
Memories linger, never lost.
Nature's voice, a tender sound,
Held by snowflakes, gently bound.

Murmurs Through the Crystal Haze

Whispers dance upon the air,
Caught in gleams of soft embrace.
Every word a hidden care,
Floating through this timeless space.

Silhouettes of dreams unfold,
Glimmers spark in twilight's glow.
Stories waiting to be told,
Murmurs linger, ebb and flow.

In the shimmering night sky,
Stars align with secrets low.
Listen close, let spirits fly,
Through the haze, their voices show.

Memories wrapped in a sigh,
Echo in each breath we take.
Moments fleeting, never die,
Found in love and paths we make.

Together in this crystal light,
Steps we take leave trails of grace.
Murmurs guide us through the night,
In this ever-warming place.

Twilight's Icy Serenade

Frosty whispers in the breeze,
Nature sings a soft refrain.
As the world begins to freeze,
Twilight casts its silvery stain.

Crystals sparkle, shadows blend,
Underneath the moon’s embrace.
Time stands still, we find a friend,
In the quiet, gentle space.

Melodies of stars arise,
Filling hearts with purest light.
Listen closely to the skies,
They weave dreams that grace the night.

In the stillness, we connect,
Lost in melodies and dreams.
Twilight's chill draws us to reflect,
On life's warmth amidst extremes.

Beneath the layers of the dark,
Hope ignites a brilliant flame.
Icy serenades leave a mark,
Forever changed, we are the same.

Veiled Tales in the Snowflakes

Each snowflake tells a story,
Whirling down from clouds above.
Silent whispers, veiled in glory,
Wrapped in warmth, like tender love.

Glistening on the ground they rest,
Softly falling, nature's song.
In their dance, we are a guest,
Hearing tales of right and wrong.

Frozen moments, crystal clear,
Capture time in fleeting grace.
Voices echo, soft yet near,
Bringing memories to this place.

As they drift, the world seems still,
Underneath their gentle touch.
Veiled tales, with winter's chill,
Carry magic in their clutch.

Gather 'round, let stories flow,
In the harmony of white.
Veiled in dreams, together we grow,
In the precious, quiet night.

When the World Holds Its Breath

In the hush before the dawn,
Time stands still, the air is thick.
Moments pause, as if a fawn,
Watches life, with heartbeats quick.

Nature waits, the silence deep,
Echoes paint the skies in blue.
In this stillness, secrets seep,
Holding dreams in waters true.

Colliding worlds, both near and far,
Rushing winds begin to sway.
Beneath the glow of a single star,
Heartfelt wishes drift away.

In the shadows, visions fold,
Every heartbeat marks the ground.
Whispers of the brave and bold,
Ride the silence, lost but found.

When the world holds its breath tight,
Hope and wonder fill the space.
In that pause, we find our light,
A moment's magic, time's embrace.

An Ode to Winter's Veil

In quietude, the snowflakes drift,
Blanketing the world in white,
A soft embrace, a gentle lift,
The cold air dances in the light.

Trees stand tall in silent grace,
Their branches clothed in icy lace,
Each breath a cloud, in crisp relief,
Winter whispers, a time of brief.

Crackling fires in hearths glow bright,
Families gather, hearts entwined,
Stories shared in the fading night,
Wonders of winter's magic unwind.

The world in slumber, peace bestows,
Footsteps crunch on frozen ground,
In this stillness, beauty flows,
Nature's canvas, profound and sound.

As seasons shift, the chill will wane,
Yet memories of winter shall remain.

The Frosted Dreamer's Essence

In twilight hours, dreams take flight,
Through frosted panes, visions clear,
A realm infused with starry light,
Where shadows dance without a fear.

The nightingale sings soft and low,
As glittering stars spark like fire,
In her song, the cool winds blow,
Awakening heart's deepest desire.

Veils of ice weave through the night,
Crystals form as time stands still,
Moonbeams cast a ghostly light,
Every whisper fuels the thrill.

As dawn approaches, dreams can fade,
But frosted moments linger sweet,
In hearts where magic often played,
In every memory, dreams repeat.

So embrace the chill, let it inspire,
The frost, a touch of nature's art.

Gleaming Whispers from the North

From the North, a gentle breeze,
Carries tales of frozen seas,
Whispers weaving through the night,
With every twinkle, pure delight.

The aurora paints a vibrant sky,
Colors sweeping, soft and high,
A dance of light, a fleeting show,
Where dreams and nature intertwine, aglow.

Footprints follow in the snow,
A map of wanderers, ebb and flow,
Each path tells stories yet untold,
In the heart of winter, adventures bold.

As the world wraps in winter's haze,
Gleaming whispers echo and play,
Laughter floating on the air,
In this serene, enchanted lair.

Let the cold embrace you tight,
For in the dark, there's hidden light.

The Stillness that Sings

Amid the silence, moments pause,
Nature's breath draws in a sigh,
Frozen stillness, without a cause,
A world at peace, the time slips by.

Gliding flakes, a soft refrain,
Each one a note in winter's song,
Together they fall, like soft rain,
In harmony, they all belong.

The gentle crunch beneath our feet,
Frost's own rhythm, steady beat,
Echoes of a tranquil dream,
In this stillness, all is gleam.

Bare branches reach for skies above,
A silhouette against the dawn,
In the quiet, we find love,
In moments frozen, never gone.

So listen close, through winter's chill,
In stillness, hearts can learn to fill.

Echoes of a Winter's Lullaby

In the quiet of falling snow,
Soft whispers weave through the trees.
Moonlight casts a silver glow,
Night wraps all in gentle ease.

Stars twinkle in the frozen air,
Each breath a cloud, a fleeting sigh.
Nature holds a beauty rare,
While dreams take flight and softly fly.

Crystals dance in icy streams,
Time slows down beneath the chill.
Wrapped in warmth of whispered dreams,
The world waits, silent and still.

Fires crackle, shadows play,
Stories told by blazing light.
In the heart of winter's day,
Hope blooms softly, pure and bright.

Lullabies of frost and night,
Carried on the winter's breeze.
Every note, a pure delight,
In the stillness, hearts find peace.

Chilled Whispers of Dusk

As daylight fades to muted gray,
Chill settles gently on my skin.
Shadows stretch and softly sway,
The night begins, the stars come in.

A breath of cold, the air is clear,
Whispers of dusk float near and far.
Through the silence, I can hear,
The world beneath the evening star.

Each petal closed, each leaf at rest,
The earth holds secrets, dark and deep.
In twilight’s chill, we are blessed,
With tales that evening shadows keep.

Crickets sing their soothing song,
Nature wraps me in its brew.
Underneath the sky so strong,
I find solace in the hue.

From the dark, a sense of peace,
Comfort in the stillness found.
As the chill begins to cease,
The whispers of dusk wrap around.

Secrets Carried by the Winter Wind

The winter wind sings through the night,
Its frozen breath a secret song.
Carrying tales of silent flight,
Of all the places it has gone.

It swirls around each bare, cold tree,
Whispers softly of dreams once past.
In its voice, a gentle plea,
To hold the moments that will last.

Snowflakes twirl and kiss the ground,
Each flake a story, unique and bright.
In the dance, the lost are found,
As shadows play in soft twilight.

A chorus of the frost and breeze,
Tales of love and hearts that soar.
In the hush of winter's freeze,
The whispers share their ancient lore.

Listen closely, feel the chill,
The winter wind will guide your heart.
With every echo, every thrill,
A journey shared, a brand new start.

Frosted Fables of the North

Underneath a sky of gray,
Fables bloom in frosty air.
With each breath, the tales relay,
Of seasons lost and moments rare.

The northern lights dance on high,
Painting stories in the night.
Whispers of the past drift by,
In colors vivid, pure and bright.

Mountains guard their ancient lore,
Hushed tales echo through the land.
Nature speaks forevermore,
With every snowflake, every strand.

Frosted trees stand tall and proud,
Holding secrets in each branch.
In the silence, clear and loud,
The myths of winter start to chance.

The moonlight casts a spell so sweet,
Fables beckon, calling near.
In the frost beneath my feet,
I find the magic, crystal clear.

Secret Reflections in Snow-lit Silence

In the hush of winter's night,
Shadows dance in pale moonlight.
Footprints whisper in the frost,
Every echo, never lost.

Beneath the blanket, secrets lie,
Crystals shimmer from the sky.
Silent stories yet untold,
Wrapped in grace, amidst the cold.

Branches heavy, bowed with white,
Dreams unfold in starry flight.
Every flake a tale to share,
Woven gently in the air.

Nature's canvas, pure and bright,
Guiding hearts through velvet night.
In this realm of soft embrace,
Tranquil moments find their place.

Winter whispers, soft and low,
In the peace, we come to know.
Breathe in deep the crystal air,
As we linger without care.

Winter's Breath

Cold winds weave through barren trees,
Whispers of the icy breeze.
Frosted windows, breath displayed,
Nature's touch, the world arrayed.

Every flake a gentle sigh,
Painting landscapes, dark and shy.
As the nightfall draws its veil,
Winter sings a tender tale.

Pine trees stand in silent guard,
Their embrace, forever hard.
Snowflakes swirl like tiny stars,
Every drift, a dance that spars.

Icebound lakes reflect the sky,
Mirrors where the echoes lie.
In this realm of crystal dreams,
Hope flows softly, like the streams.

Winter's breath, a life anew,
Blankets earth in silver hue.
In the stillness, hearts unite,
Warmth ignites the longest night.

A Soft Embrace

In the stillness, softly falls,
Gentle snow that blankets all.
Nature hushes, breath held tight,
Wrapped in warmth, the world feels right.

Every crystal, pure delight,
Cocooned in the softest white.
Here we bask in winter's care,
Moments linger in the air.

Fires crackle, warmth inside,
Hearts entwined, the chill is dried.
Laughter dances through the night,
In this glow, all feels bright.

Winter dreams in twilight's glow,
Softly swaying to and fro.
Every touch, a tender trace,
A soothing embrace, our safe space.

Beneath the stars, we intertwine,
In this moment, love may shine.
Snowflakes fall like whispered charms,
In your presence, safe in arms.

Ethereal Traces of a Frozen Realm

Glistening fields of frozen grace,
Nature's palette, a calm embrace.
Silver shadows mark the night,
Whispers dance in shimmering light.

Every breath a frosty dream,
Underneath the moon's soft gleam.
Wander through this crystal scene,
Lost in thoughts, serene, serene.

Branches arch with heavy snow,
Traces of the winds that blow.
Frosty patterns lace the ground,
In this quiet, beauty found.

Stars above like diamonds shine,
Guiding hearts with love divine.
In this realm of purest white,
Time stands still, embracing night.

Ethereal whispers softly sing,
A reminder of the spring.
As we wander, hearts aligned,
Frozen dreams, forever bind.

Echoes of Peace in Frosty Air

In the quiet of the night,
A soft whisper fills the air.
Snowflakes dance, pure and bright,
Melodies of calm, everywhere.

Beneath a blanket of white,
Footsteps crunch upon the ground.
Stars twinkle, a gentle sight,
Peaceful moments all around.

The world holds its breath in grace,
Nature's lullaby so near.
Each breath a slow embrace,
Frosty peace that's crystal clear.

As dawn breaks, colors bloom,
The sun scatters light like gold.
In the stillness, we find room,
For dreams that gently unfold.

Echoes linger in the frost,
Reminders of love's warm glow.
In these moments, nothing's lost,
Peace is found in falling snow.

Whispers in the Twinkling Light

Amidst the stars, soft and bright,
Whispers weave through the night air.
Delicate threads in silver light,
Carrying secrets, free from care.

Moonbeams dance on snowy ground,
A symphony in twinkling hues.
In the stillness, dreams abound,
Guided by the gentle muse.

Every shadow tells a tale,
Of wishes cast in night's embrace.
With every breath, we set sail,
Into realms of light and grace.

Whispers float like fragrant blooms,
Carried on the breeze's sigh.
In the quiet, hope resumes,
Filling hearts with a soft high.

Beneath the vast and starlit dome,
We find solace in the night.
In the whispers, we feel home,
Bathe in the twinkling light.

Tender Confessions from the Frozen Realm

In a world so cold and clear,
Hearts are warmed by whispered dreams.
Every sigh, a voice sincere,
Frosty whispers dance like gleams.

Snowdrop blooms in silent trust,
Soft confessions, quiet and true.
In this realm, love is a must,
Tender moments shared by two.

Glistening tears of joy fall down,
Each sparkle a memory made.
In the shadow of the town,
Hearts find shelter, unafraid.

As the frost begins to fade,
Stories linger in the air.
With each promise softly laid,
We find comfort, sweet and rare.

From the frozen realm we speak,
Words like snowflakes in the night.
In this love, we find the peak,
Tender confessions, pure delight.

Stories Carved in Icy Skies

In the twilight's gentle glow,
Stories unfold in the snowflakes.
Each flake a tale, soft and slow,
Carved in time, as the world wakes.

Above, the clouds weave a thread,
Painting pictures in icy hues.
Whispers of moments long fled,
A canvas where dreams can fuse.

Stars like diamonds start to shine,
Echoes of laughter, long ago.
In the night, our hearts align,
Under the moon's soft, mellow glow.

With each breeze that sweeps the earth,
Ancient tales begin to rise.
In the silence, we find worth,
Stories carved in icy skies.

As dawn breaks, dreams interlace,
The sun kisses snow with a sigh.
In these tales, we find our place,
Under the vast and open sky.

Murmurs in the Arctic stillness

In the quiet night, secrets lie,
Snowflakes dance, softly sigh.
Beneath the stars, whispers freeze,
Nature's hush, an ancient tease.

The air is thick with dreams untold,
Frosted stories, brave and bold.
Winds that weave through midnight skies,
Carrying tales of distant cries.

Icebergs float, proud and grand,
Guardians of this frozen land.
Echoes of life, once aflame,
Now shimmer in this icy frame.

Moonlit paths where shadows play,
Guiding creatures on their way.
Each breath a cloud, a fleeting ghost,
In this stillness, we can boast.

Murmurs blend in chilling air,
With every heartbeat, hidden care.
In the Arctic's embrace, we find,
A world of wonder, soft and blind.

Snowy Tales Beneath the Moon

Beneath the moon, the snowflakes glisten,
In the night’s embrace, they softly listen.
Whispers of dreams in winter's grip,
As shadows waltz and moonbeams slip.

Trees wear coats of purest white,
Starlit whispers fill the night.
Gentle tales of love and loss,
Written softly, nature's gloss.

Crystals form on window panes,
Nature's beauty, life remains.
In silence, hearts begin to soar,
Snowy stories to explore.

The brook flows gently, frozen yet free,
Cradled by snow, in quiet glee.
Echoes of laughter float on the breeze,
In this world, we find our ease.

As the moon hangs high, serene and bright,
We share our hopes in the soft twilight.
In snowy tales, our dreams unfold,
Beneath the moon, a sight to hold.

The Art of Winter's Breath

With each exhale, the world stands still,
A frosty canvas, nature's skill.
Whispers echo in chilly strands,
Winter's breath, in ethereal lands.

Mountains draped in crystal white,
Glistening softly in pale moonlight.
Branches bow with a heavy weight,
The art of cold, a splendid state.

Footprints trace a tale anew,
On this canvas, bright and true.
With each step, a story unfolds,
In the silence, warmth still holds.

Fires crackle in gathering homes,
While outside, the chill softly roams.
Hearts ignite with fiery cheer,
The art of winter, drawing near.

In every breath, a world of dreams,
Stitched together with icy seams.
As we gather, the cold submits,
To the warmth our spirit commits.

A Symphony of Icy Whispers

Listen close to the winter's tune,
A symphony beneath the moon.
Icy whispers dance through the trees,
Carried along by the gentle breeze.

Snowdrifts rise like soft applause,
Nature's rhythm, without pause.
Crystal notes in the still of night,
Illuminate the world in white.

Echoes of laughter blend with chill,
In this realm, time stands still.
Frosted patterns paint the air,
Delicate whispers, rich and rare.

The crackling fire's warm embrace,
A contrast to the winter's grace.
Weaving tales of distant lands,
In this symphony, life expands.

With each breath, the stories weave,
In icy whispers, we believe.
A chorus sung, pure and bright,
A symphony of winter's night.

Shadows Painted in Frost

In morning light, shadows dance,
Frosty whispers give their chance.
Glimmers twirl on silent ground,
Nature's palette all around.

Glistening trees stand tall and bright,
Beneath the veil of soft white light.
Each twig adorned, a crystal crown,
In this frosted, dreamy town.

Footsteps echo on the lane,
A soft crunch in the still refrain.
Dreams unfold in chilly air,
While shadows paint their frosty layer.

As day breaks, hues begin to fade,
Yet memories of winter's parade.
In every breath, the chill remains,
Painting shadows, tied by chains.

As twilight falls, the stars appear,
Reminding us the warmth is near.
In this cold, we find our grace,
In shadows painted, we embrace.

The Chill of a Thousand Stories

In books of old, the chill resides,
Stories whispered, where time hides.
Frozen pages, secrets told,
A thousand tales, both new and old.

With every turn, a breath of frost,
In icy winds, we find what's lost.
Voices linger, echoes sweep,
Through the pages, memories seep.

Chill deepens as the night descends,
A warm glow where the magic bends.
Huddled close, we share our dreams,
In frosty nights, nothing's as it seems.

From the hearth, the flames will spark,
As winter's chill embraces dark.
With every tale, the heart ignites,
In a world wrapped in frosty nights.

The stories weave, a tapestry bright,
In the cold, they come to light.
With whispers soft, the chill inspires,
A thousand stories, winter's fires.

Icy Cadences of Solitude

A quiet hum in winter's heart,
Where icy cadences impart.
In solitude, the mind takes flight,
In frosty silence, finds its light.

Each flake that falls, a note of grace,
In deep repose, a still embrace.
The world outside, a hushed reply,
In icy tones, the spirits fly.

Footprints mark a path now cold,
In solitude, the stories told.
Echoes ring in frozen air,
While whispers linger everywhere.

In winter's grasp, reflections dwell,
With each soft note, a hidden swell.
The chill wraps tight, a warm cocoon,
In icy cadences, life’s soft tune.

With every breath, a dance unfolds,
In solitude where time withholds.
We find our way, though paths divide,
In winter’s song, the heart confides.

Elusive Echoes in the Snow

Where silent hush meets icy ground,
Elusive echoes swirl around.
In white drifts, tales lost in time,
Whispers linger, soft as rhyme.

Every step, a story laid,
In snowflakes' fall, memories played.
The world transforms in winter's glow,
Tracing paths through a sea of snow.

Beneath the stars, the night is clear,
Where every echo can appear.
In the coolness, secrets blend,
As the shadows twist and bend.

When dawn awakes, the patterns shift,
In frosty air, the spirits drift.
Elusive echoes in pure white,
Carry dreams into the night.

As evening falls, and silence calls,
The snowy blanket softly falls.
In tranquil moments, we will find,
Elusive echoes of the mind.

Silent Veils of Winter

Silent veils of winter drift,
Covering the earth in soft white,
Whispers of the cold wind lift,
Holding secrets lost to night.

Branches wrapped in crystal lace,
Glistening under pale moonlight,
Nature's breath, a hush, a grace,
Time stands still, a fleeting sight.

Footsteps crunch on frosty ground,
Echoes fade in twilight's glow,
In this peace, a calm profound,
Nature's beauty, warm and slow.

Sparks of frost in morning air,
Dancing softly, sweet and light,
A tranquil moment, rare, so fair,
Silent veils in winter's night.

As the world sleeps, dreams unfold,
Wrapped in blankets, soft and tight,
Stories whispered, young and old,
In silent veils, through winter's might.

Frosty Breath of Dawn

Frosty breath of dawn appears,
Painting skies with hints of gold,
Every world awakens here,
Nature’s tale once more retold.

Mist that clings to blades of grass,
Whispers secrets of the night,
Sunrise paints the frozen glass,
Turning darkness into light.

Birds begin their morning song,
Harmony that fills the air,
In this moment, swift and strong,
Chasing shadows, without care.

Softly glowing, daybreak spreads,
Kissing trees with warming rays,
Life emerges from slumber’s beds,
A tender start to joyful days.

Frosty breath, a fleeting show,
Gone as quickly as it came,
Yet the heart will surely know,
Each dawn whispers nature's name.

Soft Murmurs of the Frost

Soft murmurs of the frost unfold,
A quiet world, serene and bright,
Whispers weave through morning cold,
Lending peace to fading night.

Every branch dressed in icy white,
Glistening softly, pure and rare,
Nature holds its breath in light,
Beauty cradled in the air.

Silent shadows softly play,
As the sun begins to rise,
Nature's breath in hues of gray,
Awakens dreams beneath the skies.

Frosty breath wraps all around,
An embrace felt deep within,
In this stillness, calm is found,
Creating harmony akin.

As the day begins to glow,
Frost will melt, yet memories stay,
Of soft murmurs, gentle flow,
Whispers of the frost's ballet.

Velvet Flakes in Twilight

Velvet flakes in twilight fall,
Cloaking earth with gentle grace,
Nature’s hush, a sweet enthrall,
Whispers of a soft embrace.

Glistening stars peek from above,
Drawing patterns in the night,
In this dusk, the world feels love,
Wrapped in warmth and soft, sweet light.

Each flake glimmers, pure and bright,
Dancing slowly, dreams take flight,
In this moment, time stands still,
Hearts entwined with winter’s will.

As the evening softly sighs,
Magic twinkles in the dark,
Velvet flakes beneath the skies,
Filling hearts with winter's spark.

With each breath, the world feels new,
Memories of the day unwind,
In twilight's arms, a gentle hue,
Velvet flakes and love combined.

Silhouettes on a Frostbitten Canvas

Shadows dance on the snow,
Figures lost in winter's glow.
Silent whispers in the night,
Crafting dreams in pale moonlight.

Footprints fading, memories near,
Echoes of laughter, crystal clear.
Nature's brush, in white and grey,
Painting stillness, night and day.

Frosted breaths in the cold air,
Lost in wonder, unaware.
Time stands still, as hearts ignite,
Silhouettes fade in morning light.

Threads of warmth in frigid air,
Together woven, soft and rare.
Each heartbeat, a gentle sway,
In winter's grip, we choose to stay.

Underneath this frozen seam,
Life continues, like a dream.
Through the haze, our spirits soar,
Yet in silence, we yearn for more.

Timeless Embrace of Winter’s Art

Each crystal flake, a falling star,
Drifting gently, lands afar.
Artisans of ice, they weave,
Dreams of winter, hearts believe.

Branches bend with heavy grace,
Carpeting earth, a soft embrace.
Cold winds whisper ancient tales,
Through the woods, where magic sails.

Every moment, a glimpse divine,
Capturing dusk and dawn's design.
Nature’s artistry, pure delight,
In the stillness, hearts take flight.

Frozen rivers, whispering peace,
Moments linger, never cease.
In this embrace, we lose our fears,
Warmed by hope through all the years.

Time stands still, yet flows like snow,
With every breath, the shadows grow.
As winter wraps its arms so tight,
A timeless dance, dark turns to light.

Conversation with the Icicle’s Edge

Icicles hanging, sharp and clear,
Whisper secrets for those who hear.
Glistening tales of winter's chill,
Nature's wonders, a silent thrill.

Frozen droplets shatter light,
Noise of silence veils the night.
Eager hearts, in stillness pause,
Listening deep, without a cause.

Each hanging shard, a story spun,
Of frosty nights and warming sun.
Conversations with time and space,
In the icicle's fragile grace.

Melting slowly, a quiet plea,
Changing shapes, yet still so free.
Nature's cycle, a gentle guide,
As whispers fade, we abide.

Through each drip, a sigh escapes,
Finding beauty in snowflake shapes.
Conversations linger, never end,
In the cold, we find a friend.

Glacial Secrets in Stillness

Beneath the ice, the world sleeps tight,
Holding secrets, veiled from sight.
Glacial mountains, stoic, grand,
Guarding whispers of the land.

Winter's breath, a tranquil muse,
In the silence, hearts can choose.
To listen closely, learn the lore,
Of ancient tales from days of yore.

Crystals form in elegant twist,
Nature's art that can't be missed.
Stillness wraps the world around,
In frozen peace, our thoughts abound.

Time moves slowly, yet flies high,
Underneath the vast, cold sky.
Every glimmer, every shiver,
Dances lightly on the river.

Secrets linger, whispered low,
In the winter’s gentle glow.
Embrace the stillness, hold it dear,
In glacial dreams, we find our cheer.

Shivers in the Stillness

In the quiet of the night,
Shadows whisper soft and low.
Stars above, a distant light,
Chill winds sweep through fields of snow.

Frosted branches gently sway,
Echoes linger in the air.
Nature holds its breath to play,
Silent beauty everywhere.

A lonely owl calls its friend,
Moonlight glimmers on the ground.
As the dark begins to blend,
Magic stirs without a sound.

Footsteps crunch on icy trails,
Every movement feels alive.
In the stillness, magic pales,
Yet in hearts, the hopes revive.

Whispers dance upon the breeze,
Painting dreams with frozen grace.
In the calm, our spirits seize,
Nature's pulse—a gentle place.

The Dance of Frozen Dreams

Snowflakes twirl in twilight's sigh,
A ballet spun from winter's breath.
Underneath the velvet sky,
Silent echoes tell of death.

Each crystal spark, a fleeting wish,
Whirling softly, lost in time.
A moment's kiss, a winter's dish,
In the night, we softly climb.

Ghosts of dreams glide through the air,
Whispers twine with icy streams.
A haunting lull, a tender care,
We lose ourselves in frozen dreams.

Driftwood fires burn so bright,
Lighting faces round the glow.
In the warmth of shared delight,
We forget the world below.

As dawn creeps in, the dance fades,
Leaving just the shimmering frost.
In our hearts, the joy pervades,
A treasure found, but never lost.

Hushed Cries of the Cold

Beneath the boughs of evergreen,
A stillness blankets all we know.
Softly, nature weaves the scene,
In the hush, we feel the glow.

Frosted air with tales untold,
Every breath a whisper shared.
In the gardens, silence bold,
Reminds us of the love we've bared.

Shadows cast by twilight's hand,
Dancing lightly, ghosts of night.
All around, the icy band,
Wraps the world in pure delight.

Through the dim, the heartbeats thrum,
Nature's pulse, a silent call.
In the quiet, life can hum,
Even when the snowflakes fall.

Hushed cries in the biting wind,
Promise warmth beneath the chill.
With the dawn, new dreams rescind,
Every heart, a timeless thrill.

Enchantment in White Shadows

In the twilight, shadows play,
Soft enchantment drifts like smoke.
Underneath the moon’s soft ray,
Whispers weave, and spirits cloak.

Through the snow, the magic glows,
Every flake a story told.
Nature weaves what winter knows,
In the silver night so bold.

Footprints trace a fleeting line,
Where the dreams of starlings soar.
In the air, a dance divine,
Filling hearts, forevermore.

Hushed connections, gentle grace,
Linking souls in crystal night.
In the chill, we find our place,
Wrapped in joy, an endless light.

Enchantment thrives in every glance,
As we wade through winter's breath.
In these white shadows, we dance,
Finding life beyond the death.

The Silent Tapestry of Winter's Canvas

Amidst the white, the shadows play,
In silent whispers, night meets day.
Each flake a tale, a story spun,
The tapestry of winter's fun.

Branches bend with glittering lace,
Nature's brush in gentle grace.
A canvas vast, spread wide and clear,
Winter's heart, so cold yet dear.

Footsteps echo, soft and light,
Through frosted fields, in pale moonlight.
The world adorned in icy cheer,
A moment still, as dawn draws near.

Beneath the stars, the night holds tight,
A frozen breath, a dream in flight.
Whispers hush in frigid air,
In winter's weave, we find our care.

As the sun dips low, the shadows blend,
Time stands still, no need to mend.
In every flake, a spark ignites,
The silent tapestry, pure delights.

Frosted Footprints of Time

In the dawn, where echoes rest,
Frosted footprints feel the best.
Each step whispers of the past,
A moment held, forever cast.

Crystals dance in the morning light,
Nature spins her old delight.
Every path, a story told,
Frosted footfalls, brave and bold.

Treading softly, hearts align,
In the woods, the world divine.
A fleeting touch of winter’s art,
Each frozen step, a work of heart.

Through valleys deep, and mountains high,
Frosted trails beneath the sky.
The march of time, a silent song,
In nature's quilt, where we belong.

As twilight whispers, shadows grow,
Frosted paths will always show.
The journey’s end is just the start,
In every footprint, warmth of heart.

Celestial Chants of Winter Nights

Under starlit skies, the silence hums,
Celestial chants, as nighttime comes.
With every breath, the cosmos sighs,
In winter’s grip, the magic lies.

Moonbeams dance on frosty air,
Whispers soft, beyond compare.
Each twinkle small, a tale to weave,
In the night, our hearts believe.

Cold winds carry the songs of old,
In every note, a dream retold.
The universe, a symphony bright,
Gentle hymns in the icy night.

As shadows fade, the stars ignite,
Guiding souls through winter’s light.
In each note, a soothing balm,
Winter’s breath, a tranquil calm.

Awake in dreams, beneath the sky,
Celestial whispers floating by.
Each moment pure, each silence grand,
In winter's glow, we understand.

The Hush of Icy Evenings

Evenings hush as daylight fades,
Icy tales in twilight glades.
Softly falling, snowflakes gleam,
Winter's breath, a whispered dream.

Crickets sleep, their songs now still,
Time suspends, a gentle chill.
In the air, a magic craft,
The hush of night, a soothing draft.

Trees stand guard, with arms so wide,
In their stillness, secrets hide.
A world asleep, wrapped in white,
The hush of icy, starry night.

Crisp and clear, the moon's soft glow,
Guiding paths through drifts of snow.
Each sigh escapes in frosty air,
In winter's hushed solemn prayer.

With every heartbeat, silence swells,
Within this peace, the spirit dwells.
Icy evenings whisper near,
In the hush, all hearts draw near.

Frost's Gentle Embrace

Whispers linger in the air,
Softly weaving through my hair.
Nature dons her crystal gown,
In this frosty, tranquil town.

Each blade of grass, a glistening sight,
Underneath the pale moonlight.
Branches bow with weighty grace,
In winter's tender, cool embrace.

The world is hushed, a breath held tight,
Stars twinkle in the frosty night.
Silent beauty all around,
In this magic we have found.

Footprints mark the path we tread,
Through snowflakes falling, softly spread.
A secret dance, the night's refrain,
As frost's gentle touch enchains.

Time seems to pause, a fleeting dream,
In the glow of winter's gleam.
Wrapped in warmth, the chill departs,
Frost's embrace heals all our hearts.

Reveries in Silver Shroud

Beneath the skies of silver gray,
Daylight drifts and slips away.
Clouds gather in their tranquil flight,
Whispers of the coming night.

A landscape dressed in purest white,
Each shadow cloaked from the light.
Dreams awaken, softly spun,
In reveries when day is done.

Frosted branches softly sway,
In the stillness, thoughts will play.
Stars emerge, a shimmering quilt,
As moonlight spills, the air is filled.

Hidden realms beneath the snow,
Where secrets of the winter flow.
Nature's canvas, vast and wide,
In silver shrouds we take our ride.

Moments captured, silence shared,
In this wonder, souls are bared.
Embraced by night, serene we roam,
In silver dreams, we find our home.

Hushed Conversations with the Cold

The world is wrapped in quiet white,
Where whispers meet the frosty night.
Each flake descends, a soft caress,
In hushed conversations, we confess.

Breath hangs thick in the chilly air,
Stories linger everywhere.
Comfort found in winter's hold,
As we share our secrets bold.

Branches creak with tales untold,
In the chill, we find the gold.
Silent echoes of laughter chase,
Through this stark yet warm embrace.

Embers glow, the fire’s warmth,
Wrapped in blankets, hearts will charm.
Cold may bite, yet here we stand,
Lost in dreams, hand in hand.

As snowflakes dance from skies above,
We find solace, peace, and love.
Hushed conversations with the cold,
In winter’s heart, our stories told.

Secrets Wrapped in Snowflakes

Snowflakes fall like whispered dreams,
Each unique, a tale it seems.
Crafted by the winter's hand,
Secrets whispered through the land.

Children laugh and play, they twirl,
Snowflakes swirling, a dance unfurled.
In crystal silence, truths unfold,
In patterns soft and manifold.

Nature's breath, a canvas clear,
Whispers of the heart draw near.
Footprints fill the paths we choose,
In the beauty, we can't lose.

Stars above blink in delight,
In winters' arms, the world feels right.
Secrets wrapped in each frosty flake,
Dreams await in the dawn's wake.

Frozen kisses from above,
Embracing softly, winter's love.
Each snowflake brings a truth to hold,
In this tapestry of cold.

Tender Touches of the Flurries

Softly falling, fluttering white,
Gentle flakes dance in the light.
Each one whispers, pure and bright,
Blanketing earth in a cozy sight.

Children's laughter fills the air,
Snowballs flying everywhere.
Joyful moments, hearts laid bare,
Winter's magic, a love affair.

The world slows down, a tranquil scene,
Footprints blend, like a dream unseen.
Nature's hush, a peaceful glean,
Embracing the calm, serene routine.

Branches bow with icy grace,
Silent beauty, a slow embrace.
Whispers linger, soft as lace,
Time stands still in this vast space.

As twilight falls, the stars awake,
A twinkling promise, dreams we make.
In tender touches, hearts partake,
Winter’s wonder, no heart can shake.

Ethereal Whispers in the White

In stillness deep, the world seems hushed,
Ethereal whispers, nature’s brush.
Snowflakes swirl, their outlines brushed,
Over land where dreams are crushed.

A canvas wide, both pure and bright,
Each breath visible in the night.
Stars above, a guiding light,
Magic mingles, hearts take flight.

Frozen rivers, smooth and sleek,
Beneath their surface, secrets peek.
Time stands still, the silence speaks,
In winter's arms, the soul unique.

All around, the frosty trees,
Breathe in whispers on the breeze.
Wrapped in white, our minds appease,
A moment's peace, a tranquil tease.

Beneath this snow, old stories lie,
Cocooned in dreams that never die.
Ethereal whispers, soft as sighs,
In winter's grip, we learn to fly.

The Murmuring of Frozen Pines

In the stillness of the night,
Pines stand tall, a solemn sight.
Underneath, the snowflakes white,
Murmurs echo, soft and light.

Branches sway with a gentle grace,
Whispers shared in this cold place.
Nature's secrets, time can't erase,
In frozen woods, a warm embrace.

The moonlight glimmers, shadows dance,
In the silence, dreams enhance.
Every pine a tale, a chance,
For hearts to wander, lost in trance.

Hushed by snow, the world feels near,
Every breath a silent cheer.
In nature's whispers, we draw near,
The murmurings of pine, sincere.

As dawn emerges, light unfurls,
Revealing secrets, soft as pearls.
In frozen realms where magic swirls,
The pine trees stand, as life unfurls.

Quietude Wrapped in Icy Veils

In quietude, the world finds peace,
Wrapped in icy veils, a sweet release.
Softly falling, winter's fleece,
As nature whispers, tensions cease.

Every breath a cloud of white,
The heart beats softly, pure delight.
Beneath the trees, a tranquil sight,
In the calm, we find our light.

Frosty windows, patterns lace,
Memories linger, time's embrace.
In this stillness, we find our place,
Wrapped in silence, a warm grace.

Snowflakes gather, a gentle quilt,
Filling spaces that time has spilt.
Dreams awaken, hope is built,
In this quiet, love is felt.

As evening falls, the stars appear,
Whispers carried far and near.
Quietude sings, calm and clear,
In icy veils, we shed our fear.

The Softest Tread of Winter Footfalls

Whispers dance upon the snow,
As shadows weave in twilight's glow.
Each step a secret, soft and light,
In winter's hush, a world so bright.

Branches bow with crystal grace,
The chill's embrace, a gentle trace.
In silent woods, where time stands still,
The heart finds peace, the soul does fill.

Footfalls echo through the trees,
A symphony carried on the breeze.
Where dreams are woven, pure and white,
The softest tread brings pure delight.

Beneath the moon's soft, silver glow,
A world transformed, all wrapped in snow.
In every corner, magic lies,
As winter's whispers fill the skies.

With every breath, the cold air sings,
Of tranquil nights and quiet things.
The softest tread, a lullaby,
In winter's grip, we dream and sigh.

Lullabies of Frosty Nights

Stars twinkle like diamonds far,
As the world dreams beneath the star.
The moon casts shadows, soft and long,
Singing to the night a gentle song.

Crystals gleam on every tree,
Nature's lullaby, sweet and free.
The frosty air, a soothing balm,
Wraps the earth in peace, so calm.

Each flake a note, to softly fall,
Creating magic, a shivering call.
In this stillness, hearts unite,
In lullabies of frosty nights.

Close your eyes and drift away,
Let winter's whispers softly play.
With every breath, the night unfolds,
In dreams, the warmth of love retold.

Leaves now rest, the world asleep,
Under blankets that the night does keep.
Each breath a promise, pure delight,
Wrapped in lullabies, frosty nights.

Muffled Footsteps on Sparkling Paths

Through the woods, soft footsteps creep,
Where shadows dance and secrets sleep.
Each movement gentle, wrapped in white,
On sparkling paths, a pure delight.

The crunch beneath, a whispered tune,
As nature gently hums to the moon.
With every step, the world awake,
In winter's grasp, our hearts do shake.

Glistening trails that twist and turn,
In the frost, the fires of passion burn.
While stars above keep watch all night,
Muffled footfalls tread with light.

Here in silence, magic brews,
With every step, a tale ensues.
In the calm, our dreams take flight,
On sparkling paths, beneath the night.

When morning breaks, the sun will rise,
To melt the frost from sleepy eyes.
Yet in our hearts, the echoes stay,
Of muffled footsteps on the way.

Crystalline Echoes of the Abyss

In the depths where silence breathes,
Crystalline echoes weave like leaves.
Shadows flicker, secrets sway,
In the abyss, they find their play.

Glimmers dance on darkened streams,
Reflecting softly our hidden dreams.
With every sound, the void replies,
In whispers lost, beneath the skies.

The heart feels heavy, a weight profound,
Yet beauty flourishes within the sound.
Every echo, a tale from the past,
In crystalline shards, forever cast.

As time unfolds, the darkness fades,
Light will guide through shadowed glades.
Yet still, the echoes never cease,
In the abyss, find your peace.

So listen close, for they will tell,
Of hidden wonders where spirits dwell.
Crystalline whispers, softly kissed,
In the depths, none can resist.

A Chorus in the Chill

Whispers dance upon the breeze,
Branches sway with frosty ease.
Snowflakes twirl in silent glee,
Nature's voice sings harmoniously.

In the stillness, echoes call,
Voices of the woods enthrall.
Gentle rhythms intertwine,
In the darkness, stars align.

Crisp air carries tales untold,
Every corner, mysteries unfold.
Moonlight flickers on the ground,
In the hush, our dreams abound.

Underneath a quilt of white,
Wonders hide in the soft night.
Footsteps crunch on frozen trails,
Drifting softly, winter exhales.

Together in this winter song,
We find where our hearts belong.
A chorus bound by whispered frost,
In the chill, we find what's lost.

Secrets of the Winter's Embrace

Veils of snow shroud the earth,
Hiding stories of its birth.
In silence thick, secrets lie,
Underneath the frosty sky.

Fingers trace the crystal patterns,
Nature's art, where time unfastens.
Every flake a tale replayed,
In winter’s hold, memories stayed.

Branches heavy with frozen dreams,
Echo through the quiet seams.
Whispers soft as winter's breath,
Guard the secrets, cradle the rest.

Chilled winds carry words unsaid,
In the silence, they are fed.
Time stands still in this sweet freeze,
Wrapped in nature's mysteries.

As the sun dips low and glows,
Winter's secrets start to close.
Yet in our hearts, the warmth remains,
In the quiet, love sustains.

The Frosted Dreams of Tomorrow

In the morn, the world is still,
Cloaked in white, the valley's thrill.
Dreams lie softly on the ground,
Awaiting dawn’s sweet, gentle sound.

Footprints mark the path we take,
Through the fields where dreams awake.
Each soft crunch a melody,
In winter's song, we find the key.

Stars above in silence gleam,
Guiding us in slumber's dream.
Frosted branches glow with light,
Whispering hope throughout the night.

With every breath, the cold ignites,
A spark of warmth in frosted sights.
Tomorrow beckons, bright and clear,
In every heartbeat, winter’s cheer.

As the sun begins to rise,
We chase our dreams 'neath open skies.
Frosted paths lead us away,
Into tomorrow’s bright array.

Echoing Silence of the Blizzard

Snowflakes swirl in wild dance,
In a flurry, we take a chance.
Voices lost in blizzard's breath,
Wrapped in white, we face the depth.

Each gust carries whispers near,
A symphony that draws us here.
Shadows merge in snowy haze,
In this quiet, we find our ways.

Light fades soft as dusk descends,
Winter's beauty never ends.
Caught in nature’s fierce command,
We stand still, hand in hand.

Footsteps echo with the sound,
Of dreams hidden in the ground.
In the cold, we forge our peace,
In blizzard's grip, our hearts release.

As the world transforms anew,
Snowbound wonders to pursue.
Echoing silence, fierce and true,
In the storm, I’m lost with you.

Snowflakes waltzing on the Breeze

Snowflakes dance in quiet grace,
Twisting gently in their space.
A fleeting touch, a soft embrace,
They weave a spell, a winter trace.

With every flake, a story told,
Of icy dreams and sparkles bold.
Each unique, a sight to behold,
In nature's arms, a joy untold.

They twirl like whispers through the night,
Kissing earth with pure delight.
A symphony of soft, white light,
Snowflakes waltz, a charming sight.

Upon the ground, a blanket spreads,
Cradling life in its snowy threads.
A serene hush where magic treads,
As winter's waltz around us spreads.

So let them dance, these flakes of fate,
In frosty air, they gently skate.
For each one carries love innate,
As snowflakes waltz, we celebrate.

Unseen Letters from the Sky

Whispers waft through frosty air,
Unseen letters, light as prayer.
Messages that float and dare,
To speak of wonder, everywhere.

Clouds are pages, vast and wide,
Where dreams and hopes in silence bide.
Each breeze a gentle, trusted guide,
To secrets held where hearts confide.

Raindrops drip like ink, they trace,
Stories of time, a soft embrace.
A fleeting sigh from outer space,
Unseen letters, a cosmic grace.

In twilight's glow, they fade away,
Leaving echoes of what they say.
On winter nights when shadows play,
Unseen letters, in hearts they stay.

So listen close and heed the call,
For in the silence, love stands tall.
Unseen letters, shared by all,
In dark and light, we find our thrall.

December's Soft Serenade

December sings a tender tune,
As daylight fades to silver moon.
In every breath, a soft cocoon,
A lullaby from winter's flune.

Frosted branches, shimmering bright,
Catch the glow of tranquil light.
Nature's whispers, pure and slight,
In this serene, enchanting night.

Snow blankets earth, a gentle guide,
Cradling dreams, where hopes abide.
Each flake a wish, pure love inside,
In December's arms, we'll bide.

Candles flicker, warm and near,
Filling hearts with joy and cheer.
Families gather, love sincere,
As December's serenade draws near.

So let us savor every sound,
Of December's magic all around.
In this soft serenade, we're bound,
In winter's arms, our warmth is found.

The Language of Winter's Heart

In winter's clutch, the world stands still,
A quiet peace that time does fill.
The language speaks of frost and chill,
In softest whispers, we find our will.

Bare trees sway with silent grace,
Their branches etched in time and space.
A world transformed, a frozen place,
Where winter breathes, and dreams embrace.

Snowflakes whisper, tales untold,
A frozen story, bright and bold.
In every drift, a warmth unfolds,
The language of frost, in hearts, it molds.

The crackling fires, a cozy glow,
Inviting all to share and grow.
In winter’s arms, where love can flow,
The language of heart, forever aglow.

So listen close to winter's song,
In every note, we all belong.
A shared connection, proud and strong,
In the language of winter’s heart, we’re drawn.

Tales Told on Frosted Pathways

Whispers echo through the trees,
Footsteps crunch on frozen leaves.
Stories linger in the night,
Underneath the pale moonlight.

Gentle winds carry the sound,
Of laughter lost, now newly found.
Each step tells a tale anew,
In the frost, where dreams come true.

Shadows dance, the past revived,
In quiet moments, hopes contrived.
A journey spun on crystal threads,
Where the heart and spirit treads.

The dusk begets a silent space,
All is calm in winter's grace.
Each breath forms a fleeting mist,
A memory that can’t be missed.

So tread gently on this ground,
Where stories forge and love is found.
In frosted pathways, tales unfold,
Of warmth and longing, brave and bold.

Layers of Winter's Soft Embrace

Blankets woven from the sky,
Cover fields and mountains high.
Each flake dances with the breeze,
In a world that hopes to please.

Silent nights hold whispered dreams,
Underneath the silver beams.
Softly wrapped in winter's care,
We find solace waiting there.

Frozen branches, lace adorned,
Nature's beauty, softly born.
Each layer tells a story sweet,
Of moments shared, and hearts that meet.

In the hush, the silence sings,
As the chilly air gently clings.
With every footstep, new delights,
Awakened by the frost-kissed nights.

Winter's arms hold tight and warm,
Through the cold, a peaceful charm.
In layers spun from heaven's thread,
We cherish all that winter said.

Shadows of Light in the Snow

Glistening under the sun's glow,
Shadows dance in fields of snow.
Bright reflections, crisp and clear,
Winter's magic, drawing near.

Footprints left in frosty white,
Tell of adventures, pure delight.
Each shadow holds a memory,
Of laughter shared in reverie.

As twilight falls, the colors blend,
A canvas where the dreams transcend.
Silhouettes of joy take flight,
In shadows softened by the light.

From the forest to the hill,
Time stands still; hearts feel the thrill.
What stories linger here at night?
In shadows of light, all feels right.

Here the world feels whole and new,
Every flake a whisper, too.
In the silence, peace does grow,
In shadows cast in winter's glow.

Crystalline Messages in the Cold

Sparkling gems from skies above,
Nature's touch, a gift of love.
Crystals form on every branch,
Whispers frozen, dreams can dance.

Words unspoken in the air,
Messages that linger there.
Each icy tree bears truth untold,
In their stillness, warmth behold.

Frosted windows, art displayed,
Patterns intricate, handmade.
With every glance, a mystery,
In frozen frames, a history.

Underneath the starry skies,
Lies a world where hope will rise.
Crystalline wishes softly glide,
Carried on the winter's tide.

We find beauty in the gray,
As the cold begins to sway.
These messages, so pure, unfold,
In winter's arms, we are consoled.

Frozen Murmurs in the Twilight

In the hush of fading light,
Whispers cling to the cold air.
Touched by stars, the world feels right,
Time pauses, dreams laid bare.

Moonlit shadows softly blend,
Nature's secrets softly weave.
As twilight starts to descend,
Hearts unburdened, they believe.

Silent echoes gently flow,
Carrying the night's embrace.
Frozen murmurs start to grow,
Dancing in a timeless space.

A blanket of white drapes low,
Each flake tells a story old.
In this realm where chill winds blow,
Warmth is found within the cold.

So let the night unfold its song,
In the stillness, peace ignites.
Where sorrows linger, we belong,
In whispers wrapped by starry nights.

The Quiet Dance of Winter's Breath

In the dawn of frosty air,
Winter's breath begins to play.
Each soft note, a gentle snare,
Pulls the heart in pure ballet.

Snowflakes twirl in tender grace,
Painting landscapes white and gray.
Nature's dance, a slow embrace,
Where night transforms to brightening day.

Trees adorned in icy lace,
Echoes fill the empty space.
With each step, they softly trace,
The rhythms of a silent place.

Crisp and clear, the world now glows,
As the quiet spirit sings.
Beneath winter's touch, love grows,
Wrapped in hope, on feathered wings.

In the heart of every chill,
Lies a warmth we cannot see.
Winter's breath, it lingers still,
In the dance of memory.

Drifted Memories in White

Snow drapes softly on the ground,
Whispers of the past arise.
Echoes lost, yet still profound,
Beneath the winter's tender skies.

Each flake falls like a gentle kiss,
A moment captured, held so tight.
In the silence, there lies bliss,
Drifted memories wrapped in white.

Frosted tales of days gone by,
Woven into each falling flake.
In the stillness, we can sigh,
Finding warmth in dreams we make.

Branches bow with snowy crowns,
While the world holds its quiet breath.
In this realm where time abounds,
Beauty blooms in gentle death.

So let the winter's story unfold,
In every shimmer, every light.
Drifted memories softly told,
Embrace us in this silent night.

Dreams Held in the Frosted Night

Beneath the stars, in velvet skies,
Dreams gather like the falling snow.
Whispers linger, soft and wise,
In the night, they come and go.

Cold winds carry secret hopes,
Through the dark, they drift and sway.
In this stillness, the spirit copes,
Finding light in shades of gray.

Frozen clouds, a blanket tight,
Cradling thoughts that dare to soar.
In the heart of frost, pure delight,
Awaits those who seek for more.

Each breath, a wish sent into space,
Guided by the moon's soft glow.
In the cold, we find our place,
With dreams that twirl like flakes below.

So let us dance in frosted night,
With hopes that twinkle, shine, and gleam.
In the quiet, we take flight,
Holding fast to every dream.

The Quiet Song of Falling Snow

In twilight's hush, the snowflakes dance,
Whispers soft in their gentle trance.
Each flake tells tales of silent dreams,
Weaving magic in silver seams.

A quiet tune plays in the night,
As winter weaves its pure delight.
The world transforms, serene and white,
In the embrace of the cold moonlight.

Trees adorned like crystal crowns,
Dress the earth in softest gowns.
Footsteps muffled, echoes fade,
In nature's grip, the peace is laid.

A blanket fresh, it covers all,
As laughter fades, the snowflakes fall.
In this moment, time stands still,
Captured in winter's tranquil thrill.

So close your eyes, breathe in the air,
Feel the stillness, let go your care.
The quiet song of falling snow,
Carries secrets only hearts can know.

Touch of Frost on Silent Fields

A whisper soft, the frost appears,
Like diamonds scattered through the years.
Across the fields, a glistening sheen,
Nature's canvas, pure and serene.

Morning light breaks, a gentle glow,
Painting landscapes all aglow.
Each blade of grass twinkles and gleams,
Sleeping under winter’s dreams.

A silence wraps the world so tight,
Every shadow kissed by light.
Gentle chills caress the air,
Bringing beauty beyond compare.

The earth exhales, a breath anew,
As frosty tapestries come to view.
Underneath the winter's pall,
Life waits softly, answering the call.

So roam the fields, embrace the cold,
In whispers of frost, stories unfold.
Nature's touch, so pure and fine,
In silent fields, we intertwine.

Beneath a Blanket of Chill

The world is wrapped in softest white,
Under blankets of frosty night.
Each breath is visible, crisp and clear,
In winter's realm, we have no fear.

Footsteps crumble on frozen ground,
Echoes linger, a muffled sound.
Branches bow with their heavy load,
As silence reigns, the heart's abode.

Stars twinkle hard in the chilled sky,
As time drifts gently, passing by.
A stillness reigns, the warmth within,
Nurtured by dreams where we begin.

Beneath the chill, life waits and grows,
Hidden beauty, the season bestows.
In every flake, a tale is spun,
Of quiet joy, and peace begun.

So let us gather, spirits soar,
In winter's night, we find an open door.
Underneath this blanket of chill,
Our hearts find warmth, and time stands still.

The Secret Language of Winter's Charm

In flickering light, the shadows play,
Stories whispered in soft array.
Frosted windows, a canvas bright,
Reveal the magic of the night.

Snowflakes flutter, a hidden art,
Each one unique, with its own heart.
Wrapping the world in woven dreams,
Whispers of winter in quiet themes.

Amidst the chill, a silent song,
Echoes gently where we belong.
Nature speaks in tones so clear,
In every breath, we hold it dear.

The lantern glows, casting warm light,
Illuminating the drifts of white.
In every corner, a story's told,
Of all that glitters and all that's bold.

So listen close, the secrets share,
For winter’s charm is everywhere.
In the hush of night, we surely find,
The language of joy that warms the mind.

Icebound Melodies of Night

Whispers of frost under the moon,
Echoes of shadows dance in tune.
Silence wraps the world so tight,
In the stillness, dreams take flight.

Stars glisten like diamonds above,
As the night sings tales of love.
Crisp air breathes secrets so deep,
Nature weaves its spell, we sleep.

A chill embraces the silent trees,
Their branches sway with graceful ease.
The moonlight paints the frozen ground,
In this quiet world, peace is found.

Soft flakes gather, a blanket so light,
Covering the earth, pure and white.
Each moment drips like melted ice,
In the night's heart, we find our slice.

With every breath, the cold ignites,
The spark of life in starry nights.
Icebound melodies softly flow,
In the stillness, our spirits grow.

Crystal Thoughts on the Wind

Gentle whispers through frost-laden trees,
Carries the thoughts, a delicate breeze.
Each flake that falls, a story unfolds,
In the realm of silence, wisdom molds.

Clarity dances on winter's breath,
Life's fragile notes, a song of depth.
With crystalline edges, the visions soar,
On the wings of silence, we explore.

Echoes of laughter, crisp and bright,
Wrap around us in the fading light.
Wonders of snowflakes, brief and rare,
In their short lives, beauty laid bare.

Thoughts like crystal, glimmer and glow,
Carried by winds that softly blow.
In every freeze, a chance to reflect,
To gather the dreams we dare to protect.

Moments suspended in frosty air,
Each breath we take, a whispered prayer.
Crystal thoughts swirling, wild and free,
Nature's muse inspires, endlessly.

Serenity in Shimmering White

A soft dawn breaks, draped in white,
The world awakens, pure delight.
Serenity glows in gentle light,
As day unveils its snowy sight.

Footsteps crunch on the frosty ground,
In this quiet, solace is found.
Winter's whispers soothe the mind,
A tranquil peace, so rare and kind.

Hushed landscapes stretch, silent and bold,
Each layer tells a tale untold.
Golden rays filter through the trees,
Painting the scene in quiet ease.

Clouds drift lazily, a calming sight,
Against the backdrop of purest white.
In this serene, enchanted phase,
Nature's splendor captivates and stays.

As daylight fades, evening descends,
In the stillness, the heart transcends.
Wrapped in warmth, we find our place,
Serenity reigns in winter's grace.

The Lullaby of Frozen Clouds

Cradled in the arms of soft, white skies,
Frozen clouds whisper their quiet sighs.
As twilight wraps the world so tight,
A lullaby starts, calling the night.

Warmth seeps through the frosted air,
The gentle hush of worry, a rare fare.
In the embrace of the frozen glow,
Peace flows thick, where dreams can grow.

Stars blink softly, twinkling bright,
As clouds drift lazily into night.
Their lullaby hums a soothing tune,
In the stillness, we swoon by the moon.

Cocooned in blankets of silent snow,
We listen to the world, soft and slow.
Each note a promise, a wish, a dream,
In the night's lullaby, we flow like a stream.

Time dances lightly, in rhythm and rhyme,
As frozen clouds cradle us with time.
The night wraps around like a fabled shroud,
Harmonies whisper, beneath a frozen cloud.

Silent Frosted Murmurs

Whispers dance upon the air,
A shiver wraps the quiet town.
Moonlight glimmers, soft and fair,
As shadows weave their silver gown.

The world is hushed, a lullaby,
Each breath a cloud, a fleeting sigh.
Nature rests, as moments sway,
Beneath the frost, the night will play.

Stars twinkle in a velvet sky,
Illuminating dreams below.
In gentle folds, the shadows lie,
While silence hums, a pure tableau.

Crystals form on every tree,
Adorning limbs like pearls of light.
The air is crisp, enchanting, free,
In frosted whispers, day meets night.

Each step a crunch, a soft refrain,
The world aglow with silver lace.
In winter's grasp, we feel the gain,
Of fleeting peace, a sacred space.

Veils of Winter's Breath

Veils of mist, a soft embrace,
Cloak the earth in tranquil white.
In frozen dreams, we find our place,
Where shadows mingle with the light.

The world transforms, a quiet art,
Each flake a whisper, pure and small.
In icy breath, we play our part,
As winter's call enchants us all.

Frosty fingers trace the glass,
Patterns bloom like silent song.
Time stands still as moments pass,
In winter's realm, we all belong.

Beneath the sky, the starlit dome,
We wander, lost in frosty air.
With every step, we dance back home,
To realms of dreams that linger there.

The night is draped in silver lace,
A tapestry of fleeting time.
In winter's heart, we find our grace,
As echoes soft, a frozen rhyme.

Secrets Beneath the Icicles

Secrets hide where shadows cling,
Icicles dangle, sharp and bright.
Each droplet tells of winter's sting,
In crystal realms, a world of white.

Frozen tales of days gone by,
Whispers cling to the icy ground.
As time unravels, we can fly,
Through dreams where ancient echoes sound.

Beneath the weight of quiet snow,
Lies hidden beauty, pure and rare.
A dance of light, a fleeting glow,
In secrets shared, we learn to care.

Branches bow beneath the chill,
Nature sleeps in blankets snug.
In winter’s grasp, we find the thrill,
Of cozy warmth, a softened hug.

As frost adorns the window pane,
We sit and watch the world unwind.
In whispered winds, we find the grain,
Of life that’s etched, though hard to find.

Echoes in a Frozen Slumber

Beneath the quilt of winter's night,
Echoes linger, soft and low.
In shadows deep, away from light,
The world is wrapped in silent snow.

Time slows down, a gentle pause,
While dreams drift softly through the air.
In nature’s hush, we find the cause,
Of peace that dwells, serene and rare.

In frosted fields, the silence sings,
With every breath, a story glows.
A tapestry of frosty things,
In frozen realms where stillness grows.

We wander through the icy haze,
And feel the magic all around.
In winter's grip, lost in a maze,
We find our hearts, the whispers sound.

So let the night embrace the day,
Awash in dreams of soft caress.
In frozen slumber, we can sway,
To echoes sweet, in quiet press.

Hushed Echoes in the Winter's Glow

In silence deep, the night unfolds,
Underneath the stars so bold,
Winter's breath, a fleeting sigh,
Whispers dance as shadows lie.

Frosted trees in moonlight stand,
Blankets white across the land,
Crystals gleam in soft embrace,
Nature's calm, a tranquil space.

Footsteps soft upon the snow,
Gathered dreams begin to flow,
Echoes hush, then rise anew,
In the chill, a warmth breaks through.

Stars ignite the velvet skies,
As the world in stillness lies,
Every breath, a whispered prayer,
In this winter, magic's air.

Time stands still, a fleeting grace,
In the glow of winter's face,
Hearts entwined in soft repose,
In the hush, love's echo grows.

The Hidden Lyrics of a Frozen Symphony

Notes of frost in the biting air,
Nature plays without a care,
Strings of ice begin to hum,
Winter's music, soft and numb.

Bells of snow, a quiet din,
Whispers where the cold winds spin,
Hidden tunes beneath the white,
Softly sung in fading light.

Rivers freeze, the notes collide,
Harmony where shadows hide,
Echoes lost in frosty breath,
Melodies of quiet death.

Under skies so deep and gray,
Winter holds the heart at bay,
Yet in silence, hope will bloom,
From the chill, a hint of room.

Listen close, the world will speak,
In the cold, it’s warmth we seek,
Lyrics wrapped in frozen dreams,
Carry forth the softest themes.

Snowbound Murmurs at Dusk

As daylight fades, the shadows creep,
A world transformed, in silence deep,
Snowflakes whisper, tales untold,
Drifting softly, brave and bold.

Footfall gentle on the ground,
Each step echoes, a tender sound,
In twilight's grasp, the magic swirls,
Snowbound murmur, winter pearls.

Fires flicker in distant homes,
Hearty laughter, warmth that roams,
Outside, the hush of evening's chill,
Inside, the love that time can fill.

Crimson skies and stars appear,
A canvas vast, drawing near,
Murmurs wrap the day in grace,
In twilight's arms, we find our place.

Winter speaks in softest tones,
In her flow, we find our own,
Drifting dreams in dusky hues,
Awakening the night's muse.

Glittering Fantasies in the Snow

Glittering dreams on winter's stage,
Each flake a gem, a silent page,
Dancing light in frosted air,
Whispers woven, dreams laid bare.

Sleds and laughter, joy unbound,
Footprints mark the snowy ground,
Frosty breath against the sky,
In this magic, spirits fly.

Stars descend in twinkling glee,
Gentle frost wraps memory,
Every moment, pure delight,
In fantasies, the world ignites.

Silver glows where shadows play,
Winter's heart on full display,
Glittering paths, so rare, divine,
In the chill, our hopes align.

Fantasies in snowflakes spun,
A tapestry, the night begun,
Beneath the glow, we warmly tread,
In winter's dream, our hearts are fed.

Beneath the Snow’s Silent Shroud

Whispers of winter fall down low,
A blanket soft, a quiet glow.
Each flake a story, pure and bright,
Cloaking the world, in silent night.

Branches bow under nature's weight,
A serene pause, as seasons wait.
Footsteps muffled, echoes stay,
In this realm where dreams can play.

Beneath the shroud, where secrets keep,
The heart finds peace in winter's sweep.
Veils of white cover the ground,
Where every sigh is gently found.

In the hush, the world stands still,
Nature whispers, a solemn thrill.
A canvas pure, in moonlight's gleam,
Life pauses here, lost in a dream.

Beneath the snow, the earth does rest,
Cradled warmly, in winter's nest.
Awakening soon with gentle grace,
But in the now, we find our space.

Hushed Crystals in the Air

Hushed crystals dance in the breeze,
Chasing warmth through frozen trees.
A gentle touch on skin so bare,
Nature's breath is everywhere.

Each flake a whisper, soft and pure,
In their presence, we feel secure.
Echoing secrets from up above,
They fall like tiny treasures of love.

Amidst the silence, life reflects,
In the sparkle, we find our checks.
Moments caught in fleeting dance,
Winter's beauty offers a chance.

Glistening jewels on fields of white,
The world adorned in quiet light.
We gather warmth from what is rare,
In the stillness, love fills the air.

Through frosted windows, gaze outside,
Where dreams are kept and time does hide.
Embracing the chill, hearts remain,
Hushed crystals whisper, not in vain.

The Soft Language of Winter

Whispers weave through frosty air,
Words unspoken, a tranquil prayer.
Soft footsteps mark the silent path,
In the hush, we feel winter's wrath.

Gentle murmurs touch the ground,
Where voices of the cold surround.
Frosty breath on window panes,
Tales of chill, nature explains.

In twilight hours, shadows play,
Each moment cloaked in shades of gray.
The soft language of falling snow,
Speaks to the heart, soft and slow.

Bare branches cradling the sky,
Whispering secrets as time goes by.
Every snowfall, a quiet rhyme,
In winter's chapter, frozen time.

So let us listen, hearts attune,
To winter’s soft, enchanting tune.
Its language lingers, pure and wise,
Revealing magic beneath the skies.

Gentle Touch of the White Veil

A gentle touch upon the earth,
Beneath the snow, there lies new birth.
The white veil drapes with soft embrace,
Whispering peace in its quiet grace.

Footfalls sink in silenced ground,
Nature's wonder, all around.
Each flake a silent, fleeting kiss,
In winter’s realm, we find our bliss.

Through branches bare, the stillness grows,
Beneath the cover, life still flows.
Crystalline beauty in every breath,
The calm that comes, transcending death.

While shadows dance in the fading light,
The gentle touch brings forth the night.
In twilight’s grasp, the world does rest,
In winter’s arms, we feel so blessed.

So let us wander, hand in hand,
Through this soft, enchanted land.
Where magic lingers, pure and bright,
In the white veil’s silent night.

Fragments of a Silent Storm

Whispers drift through winter air,
Shadows dance without a care.
Echoes of the night's embrace,
A quiet strength in every trace.

Snowflakes fall like silent dreams,
Carrying secrets in their streams.
They swirl and twist, a ballet bright,
Creating magic in the night.

The world transforms beneath their reign,
A soft blanket hides the pain.
Nature's peace, a treasured sight,
Calms the heart with pure delight.

In the stillness, fears subside,
As hope and wonder coincide.
These fragments weave in silver light,
Binding souls in beauty's flight.

Through every gust, the echoes play,
In stormy symphonies of gray.
A silent storm, a gentle balm,
Filling hearts with whispered calm.

When the World Falls Asleep

Stars emerge in velvet night,
Cradling dreams in soft twilight.
Moonlight spills on slumbered ground,
In the hush, pure peace is found.

The gentle rustle of the trees,
Carries whispers on the breeze.
Crickets sing a lullaby,
As shadows dance and fireflies fly.

Candle flames flicker and fade,
Illuminating love displayed.
Moments linger, sweetly spun,
Underneath the watching sun.

In twilight's arms, the world does sway,
While time slips softly away.
When dreams embrace the waking sigh,
Hope takes flight and fears all die.

So close your eyes and drift away,
To where the heart speaks what it may.
For when the world finds restful sleep,
In silence, all our secrets keep.

Tales Written in Snow Dust

On winter's breath, stories unfold,
In the crisp air, adventures told.
Each flake a page from heaven's pen,
Whispering tales of joy again.

Footsteps leave their silent mark,
In gentle trails, an arc.
Children laugh in the frosty play,
Building worlds that drift away.

Beneath the trees, old legends rise,
Wrapped in silence, beneath gray skies.
Frosty kisses on cold cheeks,
Sparkling magic everyone seeks.

A snowman stands, a friend indeed,
Of winter wonder, hearts take heed.
Each moment cherished, memories spun,
In snow dust tales, we all become one.

Through whispered winds, the stories soar,
Holding warmth forevermore.
In every drift, a precious glance,
An invitation to join the dance.

Traces of a Snowy Reverie

In dreams of white, the world transforms,
Where shadows cast in quiet storms.
A tranquil canvas, soft and bright,
Holds the traces of pure delight.

Each snowflake dances, free from care,
In the embrace of chilly air.
Silent whispers of time gone past,
In each flutter, memories cast.

Frosty windows frame the view,
As tales emerge, both old and new.
In playful flickers, wonder grows,
Wrapped in stillness, beauty flows.

Lost in moments, hearts take flight,
As echoes linger in the night.
The snowy reverie unfolds,
In frozen dreams, our stories hold.

In every corner, magic thrives,
In sparkling snow, our spirit strives.
Through every trace, our dreams expand,
In winter's grip, we take a stand.

Dreams Adrift in Silver Flurries

In twilight's embrace, the dreams take flight,
Silver flurries dance, soft and light.
Whispers of wishes, drifting away,
Carried on breezes until break of day.

Stars peek through clouds, a glimmering trace,
Each one a hope in this vast, quiet space.
Lost in the twirl of this night so divine,
I linger in dreams as the world starts to shine.

Mountains of silence rise high in the air,
Wrapped in the stillness, no troubles or care.
Floating on visions, my spirit feels free,
In the silver flurries, I'm just meant to be.

The moonlight drapes softly, a delicate veil,
Guiding my heart through this gentle tale.
With each falling flake, a new chance is born,
In this magical night where the dreams are worn.

The dawn will awaken, with colors that gleam,
But tonight, I am lost in this beautiful dream.
As shadows retreat and the morning peeks through,
I hold tight to magic, as all dreams do.

The Calm within the Snowstorm

Beneath rolling clouds, the world slows down,
A hush in the chaos, no reason to frown.
Each flake a promise, a moment to pause,
In the heart of the storm, nature breathes because.

Branches bow gently, embracing the white,
Soft whispers of winter twinkling with light.
With cotton-like silence, the world feels so near,
In this calm snowstorm, I hold the world dear.

Footsteps are muffled on pathways of snow,
Each crunch a reminder of warmth in the glow.
The air, crisp and clear, holds a magical spell,
In the calm of the storm, all worries dispel.

Dreams float like snowflakes, unique in their fall,
Each one a memory, a tale to recall.
In the dance of the flakes, my heart starts to mend,
In the storm's gentle arms, I find peace, my friend.

When the storm's fury fades, a beauty reborn,
A canvas of white greets the break of the dawn.
With a heart full of wonder, I step into light,
For there's calm in the storm, a new day in sight.

Shimmering Silence of the Winter's Kiss

Frosted trees shimmer under starry skies,
In the silence of winter, magic softly lies.
Each flake a soft whisper, a story untold,
As night wraps the earth in its blanket of cold.

The moon casts a glow on the frozen array,
Glistening softly, the world seems to sway.
In shimmering silence, time dances away,
A hush on my heart as I cherish the play.

Footprints in snow lead me deep in the night,
A luminous path where dreams take flight.
With every cold breath, I sigh and I sigh,
In this stillness, I'm lost, as the night drifts by.

Winds whisper secrets through branches so bare,
Embracing the chill with a tender care.
In the heart of the winter, I close my eyes tight,
And bask in the warmth of this shimmering night.

As dawn stretches forth with its gentle embrace,
I wake to the warmth of this tranquil place.
The memory lingers, soft, sweet, and pure,
In the shimmering silence, my soul feels secure.

Subtle Songs of the Snowbound Landscape

The landscape is hushed, a gentle refrain,
Each flake sings a note in the soft, falling rain.
Subtle songs linger on whispering winds,
In the stillness of winter, a symphony spins.

Mountains and valleys dressed fine for the day,
Covered in white, they begin to sway.
The echoes of silence entwine in the air,
A melody soft that invites us to share.

Branches sway lightly, a waltz to the breeze,
In the quiet of night, they dance with such ease.
The world hums along to the heartbeat of frost,
In this snowbound landscape, we never feel lost.

As shadows grow long, the dusk starts to blend,
With the notes of the night, the song never ends.
Underneath the starlight, together we sing,
In the soft, snowy silence, our hearts take wing.

When morning arrives with a blush on the skies,
The songs of the snowflakes linger and rise.
In the hush of the dawn, life starts anew,
In the subtle songs, I find me and you.

Snowflakes’ Silent Conversations

In the hush of winter's night,
Snowflakes dance in soft delight.
Whispers drift through frosty air,
Each one a dream, a silent prayer.

They twirl in grace, without a sound,
A tapestry of white around.
Stories told, though none can hear,
In every flake, a world so near.

They kiss the ground with gentle touch,
In their descent, they share so much.
Melodies spun in the moon's soft glow,
Snowflakes weaving magic below.

Each one's unique, a fleeting star,
Falling softly, both near and far.
Together they create a scene,
A winter's tale, serene, pristine.

As dawn arrives, the sun will shine,
But until then, let dreams align.
In snowflakes’ grace, we find our way,
In silent conversations, we sway.

Tread Softly on Winter's Canvas

Upon the snow, a quilt so bright,
Footprints etch the soft twilight.
Nature's canvas, pure and wide,
Whispers of the world inside.

Each step a mark, a fleeting sign,
With care we lace our path divine.
Around us, shadows softly play,
In winter's grasp, they drift away.

The trees stand tall, wrapped in white,
Guardians of this tranquil night.
The air is crisp, a gentle chill,
As frosted dreams begin to fill.

So tread with love, embrace the cold,
Winter's stories yet untold.
In silence found, a peace so rare,
On winter's canvas, we lay bare.

Each breath a frosty cloud unfurls,
Beneath the sky, a quiet world.
With every step, we find our way,
In winter's beauty, here we stay.

Beneath the Crystal Canopy

Beneath the trees, where crystals cling,
A sparkling world, where echoes ring.
Branches bowed with weighty grace,
In winter's hall, a sacred space.

Each droplet shines, a gem in light,
Nature's art in purest sight.
The whispering winds through needles flow,
A timeless dance, the softest glow.

In slumber deep, the world awaits,
Wrapped in peace, as daylight fades.
Tranquil moments, the heart will seek,
In winter's breath, the spirit speaks.

Footsteps gentle on the ground,
A silence vast, a soothing sound.
Beauty glimmers, a fleeting dream,
Beneath the canopy's gentle gleam.

As shadows lengthen, dusk unfolds,
Wrapped in tales of winter's holds.
We linger here, our worries rest,
In crystal haven, we are blessed.

The Soft Whisper of Falling White

A hush descends, the world in white,
Snowflakes drifting through the night.
Softly whispered, they come to rest,
A blanket warm, nature's best.

In quiet spirals, they glide down,
Transforming earth to a jeweled gown.
Each flake unique, a story spun,
In fleeting moments, they are one.

The air is filled with gentle sighs,
As winter breathes beneath the skies.
Frosted whispers touch the ground,
In every flake, a peace is found.

Time seems to pause in falling snow,
A dance of dreams, both soft and slow.
With every flurry, hope takes flight,
In the soft whispers of falling white.

Embrace the chill, let worries cease,
In winter's hush, discover peace.
As silence reigns, hearts will align,
In the magic of the snow's design.

Milton Keynes UK
Ingram Content Group UK Ltd.
UKHW021045031224
452078UK00010B/593

9 789916 797549